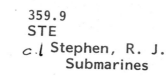

DATE DUE			

DEMCO

Franklin Watts Inc
387 Park Avenue South
New York
NY 10016

Library of Congress Cataloging-in-Publication Data
Stephen, R. J.
    Submarines / R. J. Stephen.
        p.   cm. — (Picture world)
    Includes index.
    Summary: Describes the role of various types of submarines in
modern warfare.
    ISBN 0-531-14011-3
    1. Submarine boats—Juvenile literature.   2. Submarine warfare—
—Juvenile literature.   [1. Submarines.   2. Submarine warfare.]
    I. Title.   II. Series.
    V210.B32   1990
    359.9'6—dc20

89-36532
CIP
AC

Series Editor
Norman Barrett

Designed by
K & Co

Photographs by
ECP Armées
Fleet Photographic Unit
Royal Navy Submarine Museum
U.S. Navy
U.S. Department of Defense
N.S. Barrett

Technical Consultant
Bernie Fitzsimons

The Picture World of
Submarines

R.J. Stephen

CONTENTS

Franklin Watts

London • New York • Sydney • Toronto

Introduction

Submarines are warships that operate underwater. These stealthy boats fire their deadly weapons from below the waves.

There are different kinds of submarines. The most powerful use nuclear fuel and can stay submerged for months at a time. Smaller submarines run on diesel fuel and have to come to the surface to "breathe."

▽ A nuclear-powered submarine on the surface. The structure rising from the body of the boat is the fin, or sail. It houses periscopes and antennas, and is used as an observation platform when the submarine is on the surface.

◁ A submarine prepares to dive. Submarines are faster underwater than on the surface.

▽ An officer looks through the periscope. Periscopes are used to scan wide areas of the ocean while the submarine is just under the surface.

Under the water

The body, or hull, of a submarine has an inner and an outer shell. Between the two shells are spaces that hold water. These are the ballast, or buoyancy, tanks.

To enable a submarine to dive, sea water is allowed into the ballast tanks. For going up again, compressed air is forced into the tanks, driving out the water.

△ A nuclear submarine shoots up through the water in an emergency surfacing drill, with water pouring from her ballast tanks. A normal ascent is more gradual.

Conventional submarines are diesel-powered. Below the surface, they run on electricity produced by batteries. They use their diesel engines to travel on the surface and to recharge their batteries. Their engines need air and work only on or near the surface.

Nuclear-powered submarines do not need to surface except for taking on supplies. A tiny amount of uranium can keep a submarine's nuclear reactor working for years.

▽ A nuclear-powered submarine sticks up through the ice at the North Pole.

Living underwater

Nuclear submarines have a crew of 100 or more men, including about 12 officers. They usually work in "watches" of four hours at a time. A tour of duty might last for two months or more. Then a completely new crew take over.

A submarine's crew are highly trained. They have to live in an enclosed space for long periods of time, cut off from the outside world.

▽ The mess, where the crew take their meals.

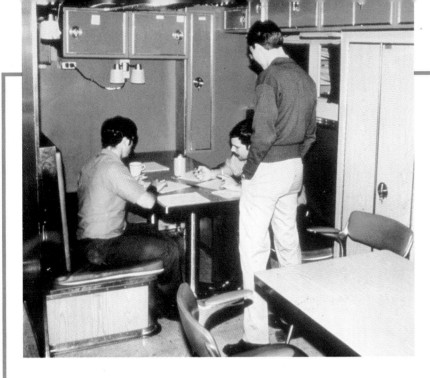

◁ The crew relax in a lounge on the third level of a ballistic missile submarine. This is located in the compartment that also contains the deadly nuclear weapons.

▷ A technician mans his station in the sonar room. Sonar is a method of detecting objects by means of sound echoes. It is how a submarine "sees" underwater.

◁ The missile control room in a ballistic missile submarine. The devastation to the world that would be caused if the 24 nuclear weapons were ever launched is terrifying.

On the surface

Submarines spend most of their time underwater, where they are difficult to detect. On the surface, a submarine performs like other types of warship. Nuclear submarines have a surface cruising speed of about 20 knots (37 km/h, 23 mph), conventional submarines less than this.

▷ Crewmen on USS *Scamp*. Hydroplanes, used for maneuvering the submarine underwater, serve as observation platforms when it is on the surface.

▽ USS *Guardfish* underway.

Hunter-killer submarines

Hunter-killer submarines, sometimes called attack submarines, are used for attacking enemy submarines. They are also called fleet submarines, because they are often attached to a fleet of ships. They help to protect aircraft carriers from enemy submarines.

Hunter-killers are powered by nuclear fuel. They are armed with missiles and torpedoes.

△ HMS *Tireless*, a hunter-killer of the British Navy.

▷ The USS *Atlanta* is launched in a colorful ceremony. It belongs to the Los Angeles class, most of which bear the names of American cities.

◁ USS *Sturgeon* underway. There are 37 submarines in the Sturgeon class, most of them with names of fish or other sea creatures.

▽ HMS *Swiftsure* in port. The six Swiftsure class submarines all have names beginning with the letter S.

Hunter-killer submarines provide the major navies of the world with their greatest power. They attack other submarines and are the deadly enemy of surface ships. They can cripple an aircraft carrier with torpedoes. Some hunter-killer submarines can fire cruise missiles at ships over the horizon. The missiles may be guided to their target by high-flying aircraft or satellites.

△ HMS *Trafalgar* rises to the surface. British submarines with names beginning with T all belong to the seven-strong Trafalgar class.

△ USS *Snook* putting into the port of Rio, in Brazil. The occasional visit to other ports makes life more interesting for the crew of an attack submarine, which spends long periods underwater, away from its home port.

▷ Crewmen use binoculars to search the seas as they stand in front of raised periscopes on the fin of the USS *City of Corpus Christi*.

△ A Soviet Alpha class hunter-killer, said to be faster than any other class of submarine.

Only the Soviet Navy has more attack submarines than the U.S. Navy, although little is known about them.

◁ A rare glimpse of a Soviet Victor III class attack submarine, in difficulty off the North Carolina coast.

Ballistic missile submarines

Ballistic missile submarines are the largest underwater warships. They carry as many as 24 long-range nuclear missiles.

Most of the world's SSBNs, as they are called, belong to the navies of the United States and the Soviet Union. The British, French and Chinese navies also operate a few SSBNs.

▽ HMS *Repulse*, a Resolution class SSBN of the British Navy.

△ USS *Casimir Pulaski,* a Lafayette class SSBN of the U.S. Navy.

▷ The hydroplanes of the USS *Georgia* are covered in ice as the vessel comes into a North Atlantic port in winter.

The SSBN has an entirely different role from the hunter-killer. Its job is to lie hidden in the depths of the ocean, undetected by the enemy.

Its weapons are not for waging war on the seas. They act as a threat to an opposing power that might start a nuclear war.

Over a hundred SSBNs lurk in the world's oceans, with enough power to obliterate life on earth several times over.

▽ A ballistic missile submarine of the Soviet Navy, one of the Golf II class. Known as SSBs, these vessels are non-nuclear, being powered by diesel fuel—but they carry nuclear missiles.

The SSBN carries about 150 men. They all have their jobs to do, and are kept occupied with drills and exercises.

It is an unusual life, however, preparing for something they hope will never happen. The crew might spend half a day getting the missiles ready for launching. But if they ever were launched, there would probably be no world to return to above water.

△ The crew in the control room of the USS *Ohio* go through a missile firing drill.

Patrol submarines

Patrol submarines are diesel-powered. Their job is to attack enemy shipping. They are slower than nuclear-powered submarines and must come up to the surface for air at regular intervals.

Most of the world's navies operate patrol submarines. They are much cheaper to build than nuclear submarines and need a smaller crew.

▷ An unusual view of HMS *Onslaught* as it plows through the waves. Like most other diesel-electric submarines, the surface speed of this Oberon class boat is only about 12 knots (13$\frac{1}{2}$ mph), and its underwater speed 17 knots (19 mph).

▽ The *Agosta* is a French patrol submarine.

Facts

Submersibles

Small vessels used for underwater research or maintenance work are called submersibles. Some are unmanned while others have a crew of up to three.

An Italian-built submersible called the *Trieste*, bought by the U.S. Navy for underwater research, has been taken down to the deepest part of the oceans. This is known as the Challenger Deep, and its floor is 36,000 feet (10,900 meters) below sea level.

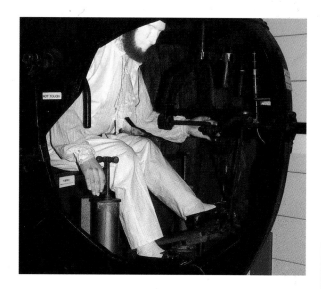

△ A cut-away model of the *Turtle*, which was driven by a propeller cranked by hand.

△ The deep-diving submersible *Trieste*.

The first attack

The first underwater attack on a warship was made by the *Turtle*, a one-man submarine. This curious machine was built in the 1770s by David Bushnell, a student at Yale College, for use in the American War of Independence. Piloted by Sergeant Ezra Lee, the *Turtle* attacked a British warship blockading New York harbor. But he was unable to release the only weapon, a mine, so the attack failed.

Speed and size

The fastest submarines belong to the Alpha class operated by the Soviet Navy. They are said to reach an underwater speed of 43 knots (50 mph).

The largest submarines are the SSBNs, with their cargo of nuclear missiles. The Soviet Typhoon class SSBNs are about 600 ft (183 m) long.

Deep Sea Rescue

A special kind of rescue vessel is operated by the U.S. Navy for evacuating the crew of a submerged submarine in difficulties. The Deep Submergence Rescue Vessel, or DSRV, is about 49 ft (15 m) long and can carry up to 24 survivors. It is transported by ship or submarine to the scene of the emergency, and locks onto a rescue hatch on the submarine in trouble.

△ A Soviet Yankee class SSBN in trouble on the Atlantic after an explosion on board. The submarine sank three days later.

The City of Corpus Christi

Most of the Los Angeles class hunter-killer submarines are named after American cities. Corpus Christi, in Texas, is the headquarters of the Naval Air Training Command. But the submarine named after it had to change its name to *City of Corpus Christi*, because Corpus Christi means "body of Christ." This was thought to be an unsuitable name for a ship of war.

△ The submarine USS *Pintado,* underway with a DSRV attached on top during a rescue drill.

Glossary

Ballast tanks
Spaces in the outer structure of a submarine into which water or air is allowed according to whether the vessel is going down or rising.

Ballistic missile submarine
A submarine armed with long-range nuclear missiles.

Conventional submarine
A submarine that runs on diesel-electric power.

Diesel-electric submarine
A conventional submarine, using diesel fuel to provide electricity.

Fin
The structure that houses the periscopes and antennas.

Hunter-killer
A nuclear submarine whose main duties are to attack the enemy and protect ships of its own fleet.

Hydroplanes
Small wings that stick out from both sides of the fin and the stern (back) of a submarine. They are used for guiding the boat underwater.

Knot
One nautical mile per hour. One knot equals 1.15 mph.

Nuclear reactor
A device that generates energy by means of atomic reactions.

Patrol submarine
A small, diesel-powered submarine whose task is to attack enemy ships.

Sonar
A means for detecting objects under the water by echoes.

SSBN
A nuclear-powered ballistic missile submarine.

Uranium
A metal used as nuclear fuel. It provides more than two million times as much energy as the equivalent amount of coal.

Index